HAL•LEONARD

BASS PLAY-ALONG

ROCKBAND

T0081965

Tracking, mixing, and mastering by
Jake Johnson & Bill Maynard at Paradyme Productions
Bass by Tom McGirr
Guitars by Doug Boduch
Keyboards by Warren Wiegratz
Drums by Scott Schroedl

ISBN 978-1-4234-4025-3

HAL•LEONARD®
CORPORATION
7777 W. BLUEMOUND RD. P.O. BOX 13819 MILWAUKEE, WI 53213

Visit Hal Leonard Online at
www.halleonard.com

ROCKBAND™

VOL. 22

ROCKBAND

CONTENTS

Bass Notation Legend

Bass music can be notated two different ways: on a *musical staff,* and in *tablature*

THE MUSICAL STAFF shows pitches and rhythms and is divided by bar lines into measures. Pitches are named after the first seven letters of the alphabet.

TABLATURE graphically represents the bass fingerboard. Each horizontal line represents a string, and each number represents a fret.

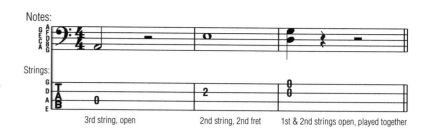

3rd string, open   2nd string, 2nd fret   1st & 2nd strings open, played together

---

HAMMER-ON: Strike the first (lower) note with one finger, then sound the higher note (on the same string) with another finger by fretting it without picking.

PULL-OFF: Place both fingers on the notes to be sounded. Strike the first note and without picking, pull the finger off to sound the second (lower) note.

LEGATO SLIDE: Strike the first note and then slide the same fret-hand finger up or down to the second note. The second note is not struck.

SHIFT SLIDE: Same as legato slide, except the second note is struck.

TRILL: Very rapidly alternate between the notes indicated by continuously hammering on and pulling off.

TREMOLO PICKING: The note is picked as rapidly and continuously as possible.

VIBRATO: The string is vibrated by rapidly bending and releasing the note with the fretting hand.

SHAKE: Using one finger, rapidly alternate between two notes on one string by sliding either a half-step above or below.

NATURAL HARMONIC: Strike the note while the fret hand lightly touches the string directly over the fret indicated.

MUFFLED STRINGS: A percussive sound is produced by laying the fret hand across the string(s) without depressing them and striking them with the pick hand.

BEND: Strike the note and bend up the interval shown.

BEND AND RELEASE: Strike the note and bend up as indicated, then release back to the original note. Only the first note is struck.

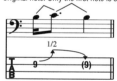

RIGHT-HAND TAP: Hammer ("tap") the fret indicated with the "pick-hand" index or middle finger and pull off to the note fretted by the fret hand.

LEFT-HAND TAP: Hammer ("tap") the fret indicated with the "fret-hand" index or middle finger.

SLAP: Strike ("slap") string with right-hand thumb.

POP: Snap ("pop") string with right-hand index or middle finger.

Additional Musical Definitions

 (accent) • Accentuate note (play it louder)

 (accent) • Accentuate note with great intensity

 (staccato) • Play the note short

D.S. al Coda • Go back to the sign (𝄋), then play until the measure marked *"To Coda,"* then skip to the section labelled *"Coda."*

Fill • Label used to identify a brief pattern which is to be inserted into the arrangement.

 • Repeat measures between signs.

 • When a repeated section has different endings, play the first ending only the first time and the second ending only the second time.

Ballroom Blitz

Words and Music by Mike Chapman and Nicky Chinn

hard liv-in' with the things ___ you do ___ to me. ___

Uh, huh. ___

My dreams are get-tin' so ___ strange, I'd

like to tell you ev-'ry-thing I see. Mm.

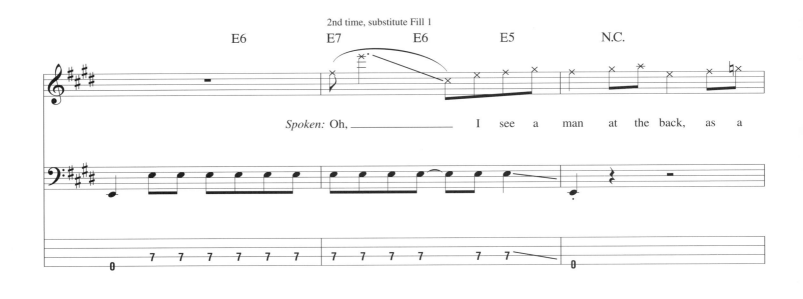

Spoken: Oh, _____ I see a man at the back, as a

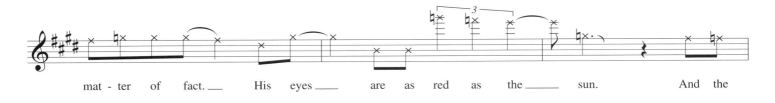

mat - ter of fact. _____ His eyes _____ are as red as the _____ sun. And the

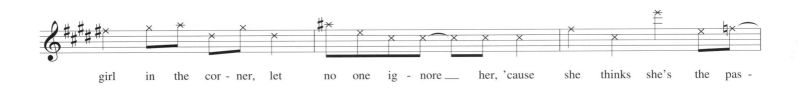

girl in the cor - ner, let no one ig - nore _____ her, 'cause she thinks she's the pas -

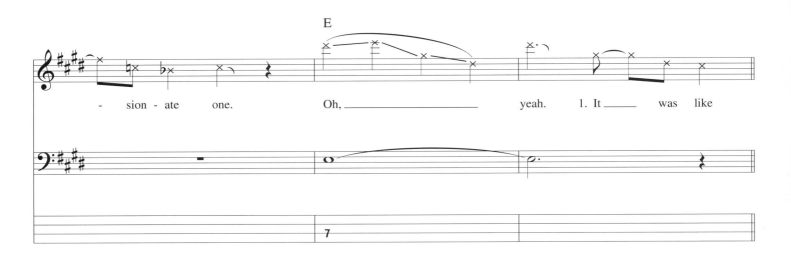

- sion - ate one. Oh, _____ yeah. 1. It _____ was like

Fill 1

%.% Pre-Chorus

(3.) light - ning. ___
2. *See additional lyrics*

Ev - 'ry - bod - y was fright - 'ning, ___

and the mu - sic was sooth - ing, _____ and they all start - ed ___

2nd & 3rd times, substitute Fill 2

___ groov - ing. Yeah, yeah, yeah, yeah, yeah. And the

Fill 2

Additional Lyrics

2. Oh, I'm reachin' out for something; touching nothing's all I ever do.
Oh, I softly call you over. When you appear, there's nothing left of you. Uh, huh.
Now the man at the back is ready to crack as he raises his hands to the sky.
And the girl in the corner is ev'ryone's mourner; she could kill you with a wink of her eye.
Oh, yeah.

Pre-Chorus 2. It was electric, so frantic'ly hectic,
And the band started leaping 'cause they all stopped breathing.
Yeah, yeah, yeah, yeah, yeah.

Should I Stay or Should I Go

Words and Music by Mick Jones and Joe Strummer

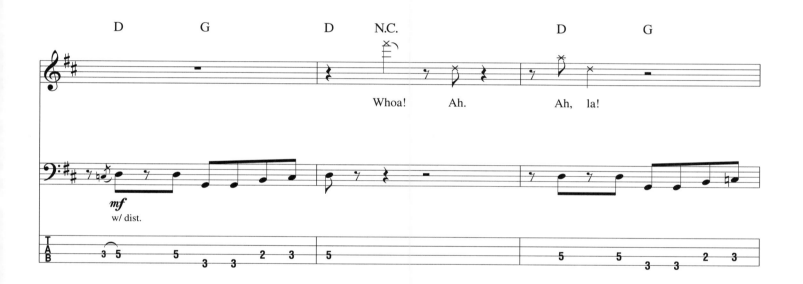

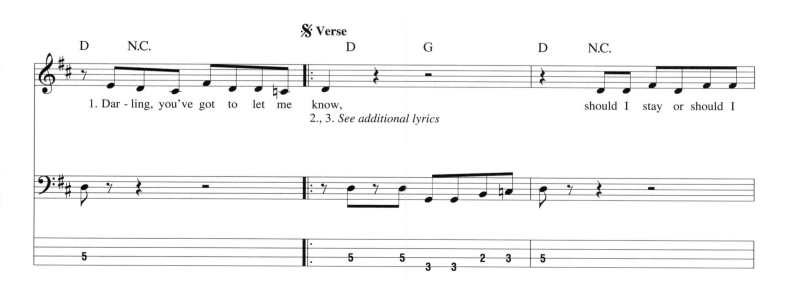

To Coda ⊕

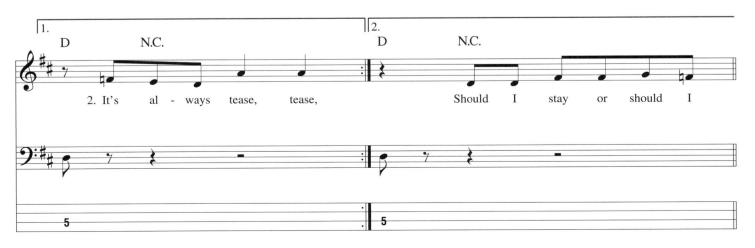

Chorus
Double-time feel

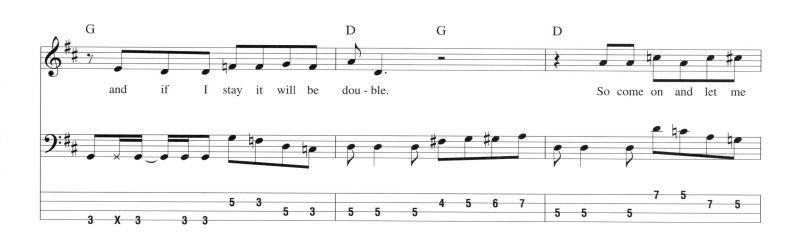

D.S. al Coda
End double-time feel

15

Ah!

Split.

Yo me fri-o per lo so-plo!)

know, _____ should I cool it or should I

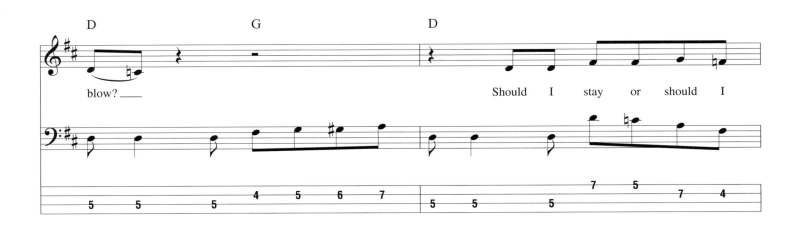

blow? ____ Should I stay or should I

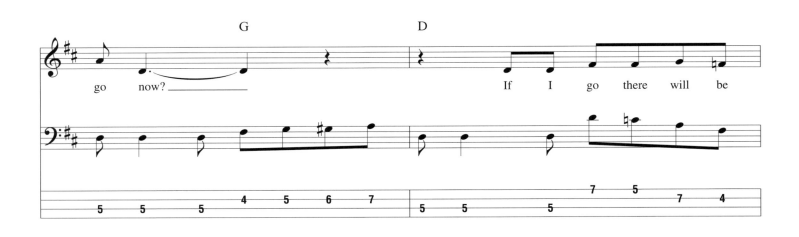

go now? _____ If I go there will be

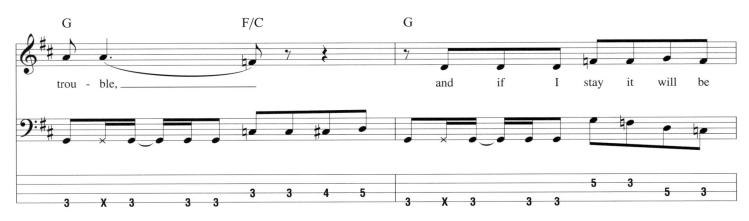

trou - ble, _____ and if I stay it will be

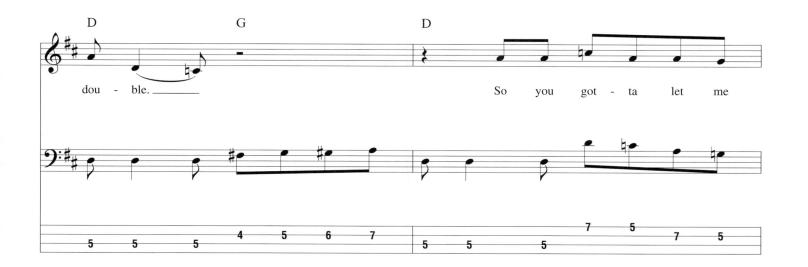

dou - ble. _____

So you got - ta let me

End double-time feel

know, _____

should I stay or should I go?

Additional Lyrics

2. It's always tease, tease, tease.
   You're happy when I'm on my knees.
   One day is fine and next it's black.
   So if you want me off your back,
   Well, come on and let me know:
   Should I stay or should I go?

3. This indecision's buggin' me.
   If you don't want me, set me free.
   Exactly who I'm s'pose to be?
   Don't you know which clothes even fit me?
   Come on and let me know:
   Should I cool it or should I blow?

Detroit Rock City

Words and Music by Paul Stanley and Bob Ezrin

Tune down 1/2 step:
(low to high) Eb-Ab-Db-Gb

feel up-tight on a Sat-ur-day night. __
2., 3. *See additional lyrics*

Nine o'-clock, the ra-di-o's the on-ly light. __

Coda

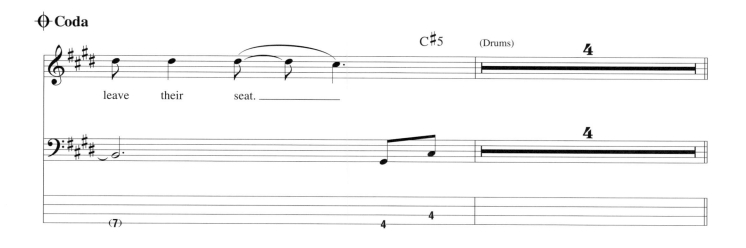

leave their seat. _____

Interlude

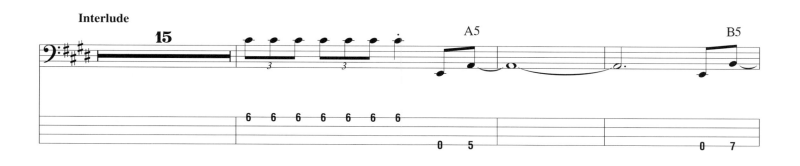

You got-ta lose your life in De - troit Rock

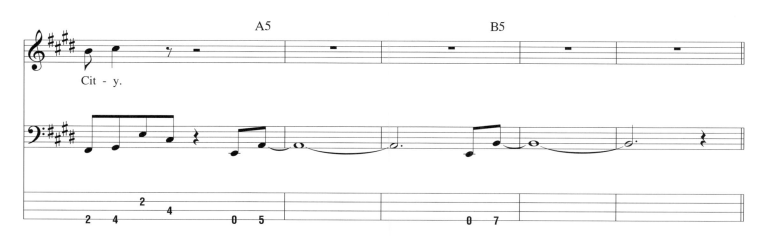

Cit - y.

Chorus

Ev-'ry-bod-y's gon-na move their feet.

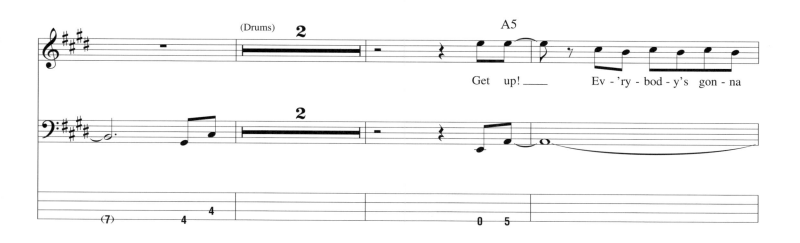

(Drums)

Get up! Ev-'ry-bod-y's gon-na

leave their seat, get down!

Additional Lyrics

2. Gettin' late, I just can't wait.
   Ten o'clock, and I know I gotta hit the road.
   First I drink, then I smoke.
   Start up the car, and I try to make the midnight show.

3. Movin' fast down Ninety-Five.
   Hit top speed, but I'm still movin' much too slow.
   I feel so good; I'm so alive.
   Hear my song playin' on the radio.
   It goes:

Don't Fear the Reaper

Words and Music by Donald Roeser

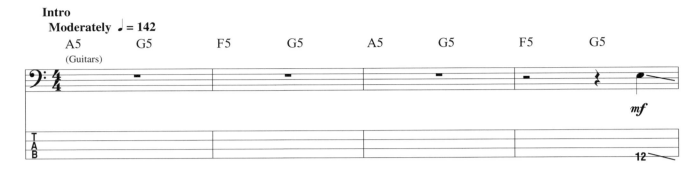

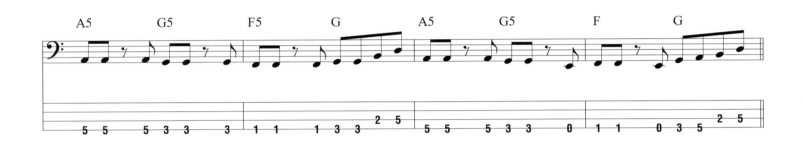

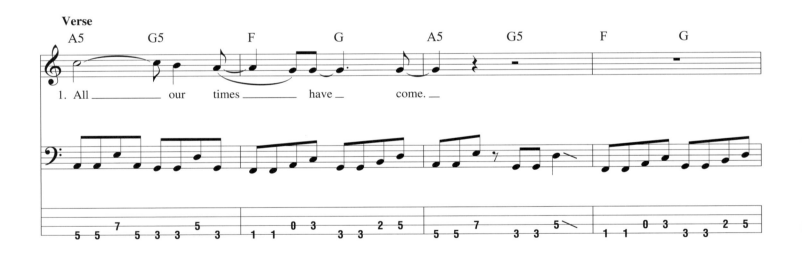

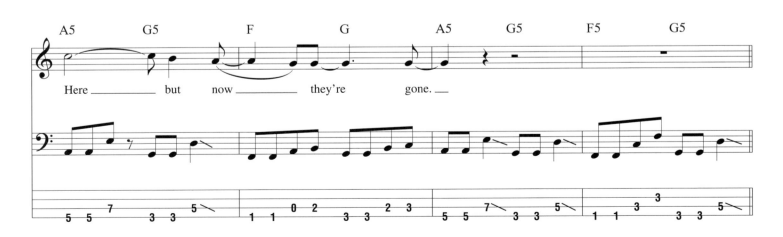

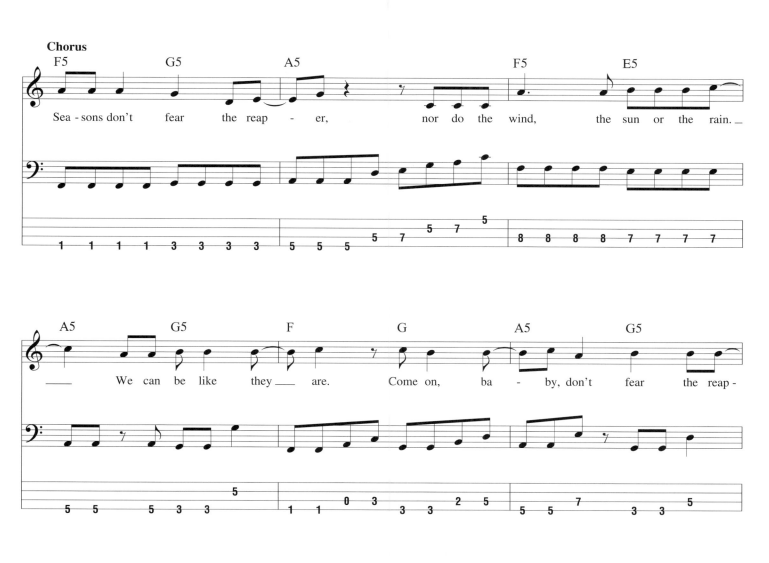

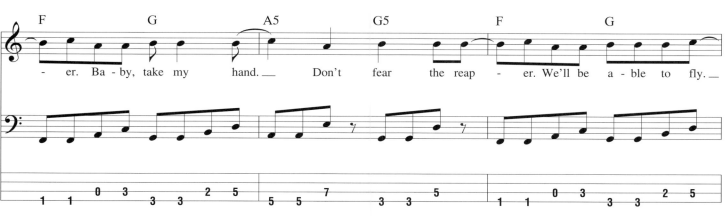

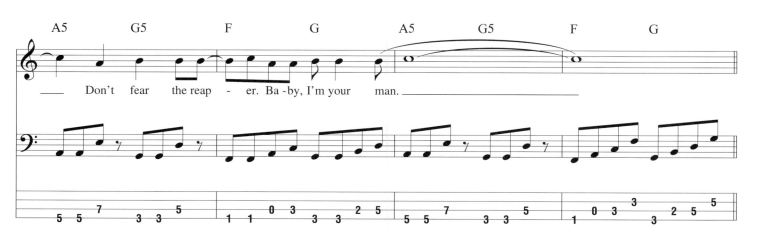

Interlude

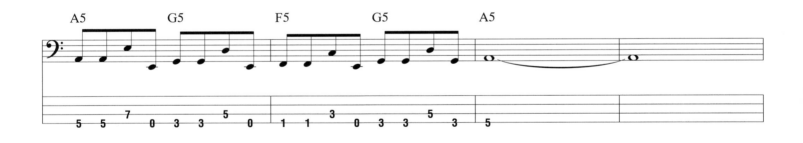

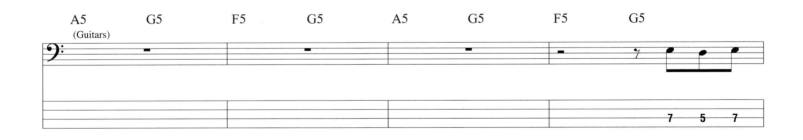

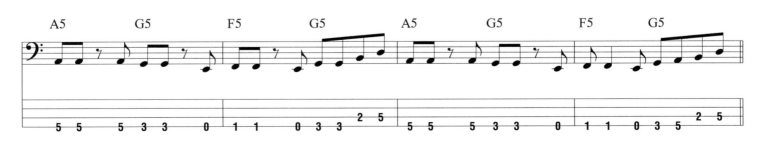

Interlude

La, _____ la, la, _____ la, ___ la.

La, _____ la, la, _____ la, ___ la.

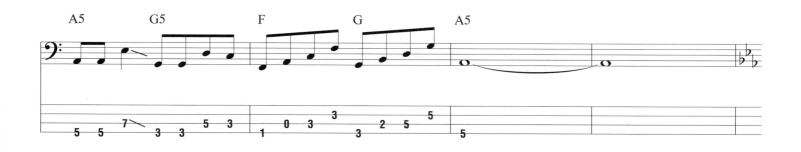

Bass tacet

Guitar Solo

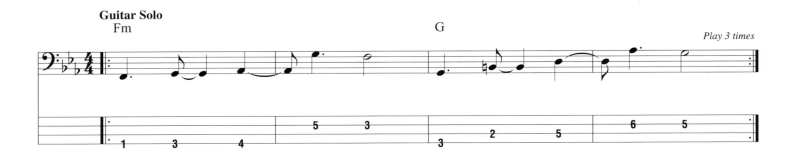

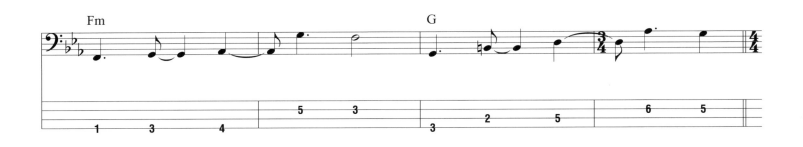

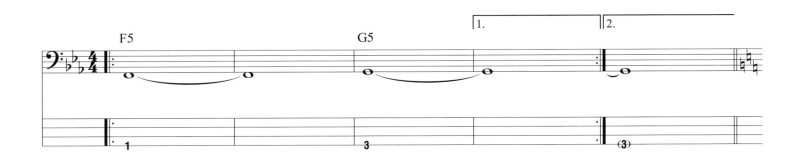

Interlude

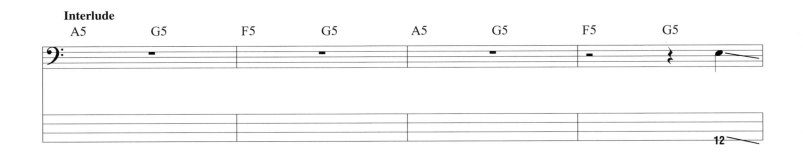

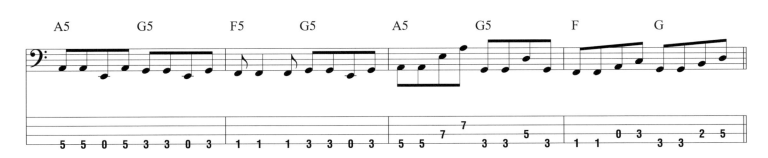

32

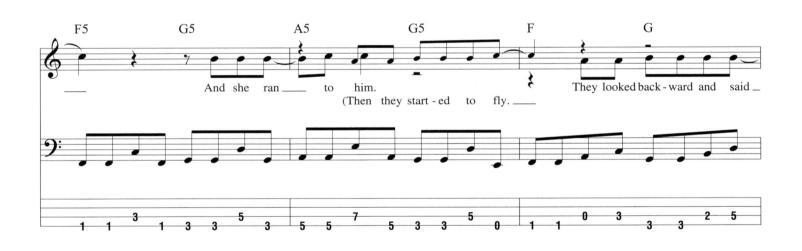

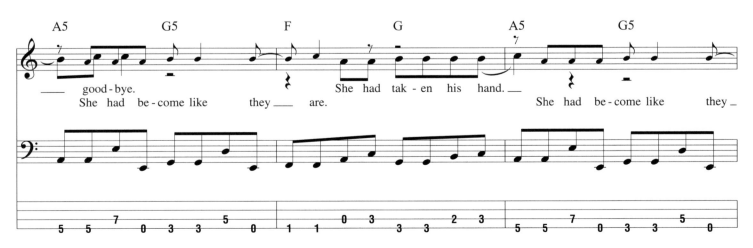

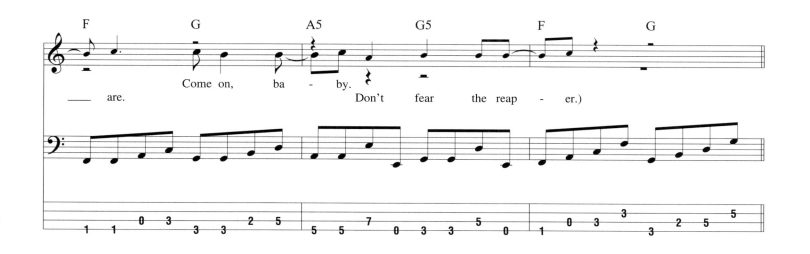

Come on, ba - by.
__ are. Don't fear the reap - er.)

Outro

Play 4 times

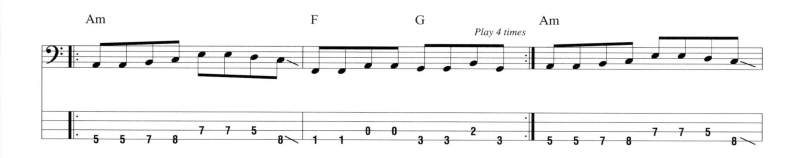

Play 4 times and fade

Highway Star

Words and Music by Ritchie Blackmore, Ian Gillan, Roger Glover, Jon Lord and Ian Paice

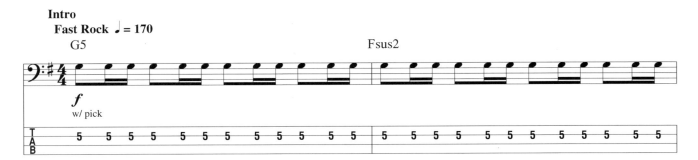

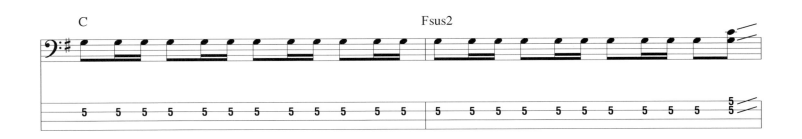

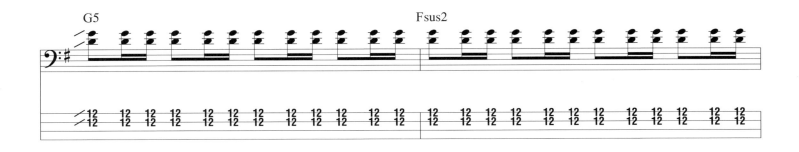

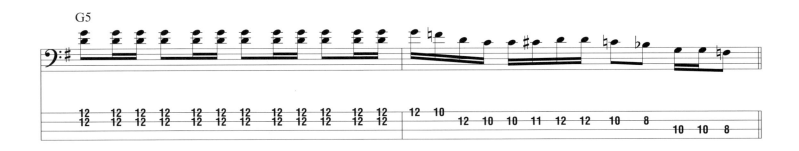

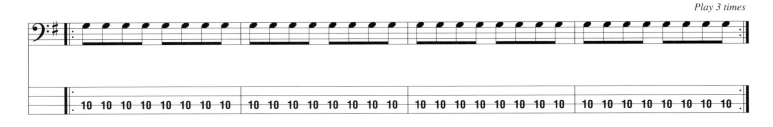

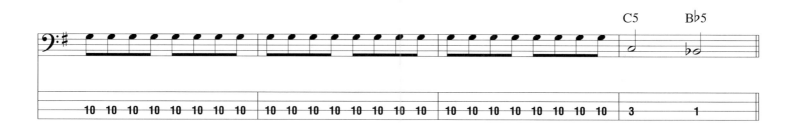

§ Verse

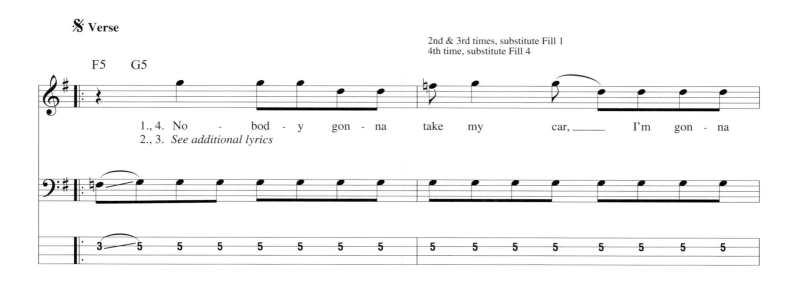

2nd & 3rd times, substitute Fill 1
4th time, substitute Fill 4

1., 4. No - bod - y gon - na take my car, _____ I'm gon - na
2., 3. *See additional lyrics*

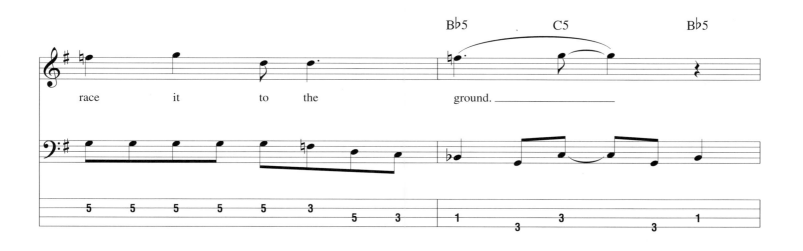

race it to the ground. _____

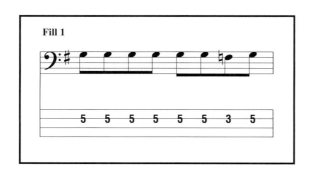

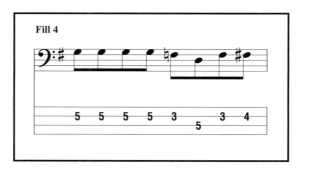

2nd time, substitute Fill 1
4th time, substitute Fill 5

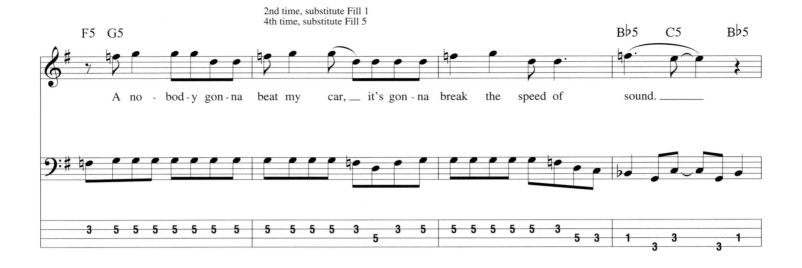

A no-bod-y gon-na beat my car, __ it's gon-na break the speed of sound. __

Ooh, _____ it's a kill-in' ma-chine, __ it's got, a, ev-'ry-thing. __

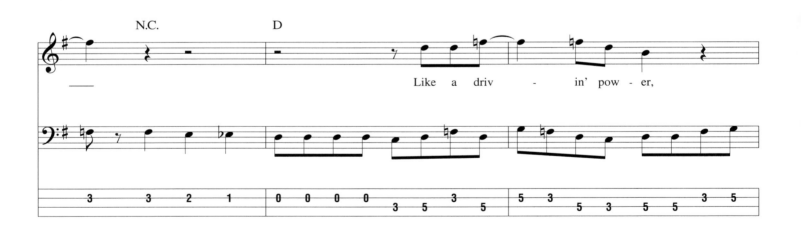

__ Like a driv - in' pow - er,

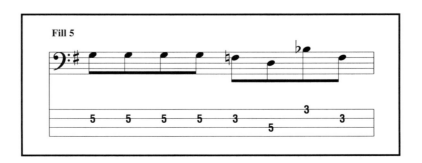

Fill 5

2nd time, substitute Fill 2
3rd time, substitute Fill 3
4th time, substitute Fill 6

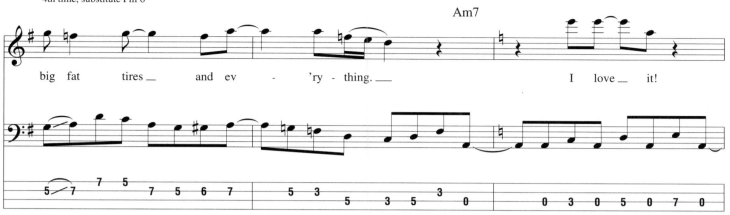

big fat   tires ___   and ev - 'ry - thing. ___   I love ___ it!

And I need __ it!   I   bleed __ it!

Fill 2

Fill 3

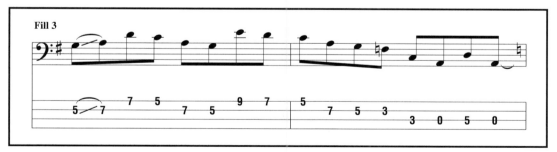

Fill 6

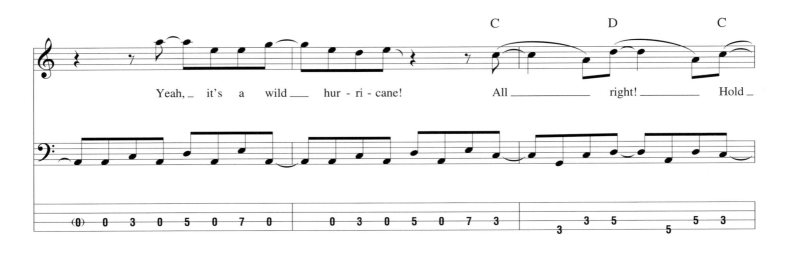

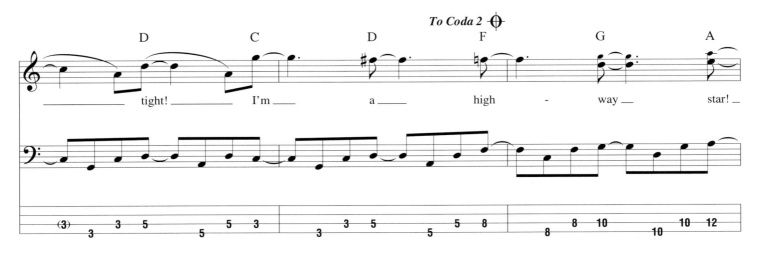

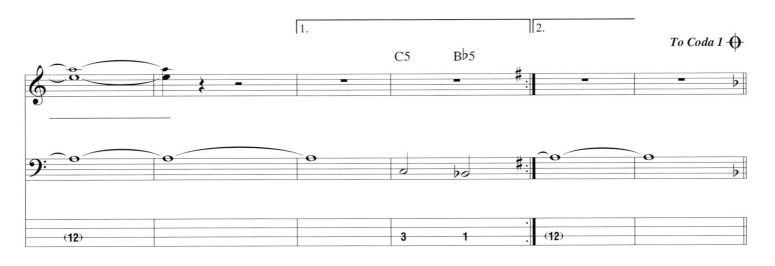

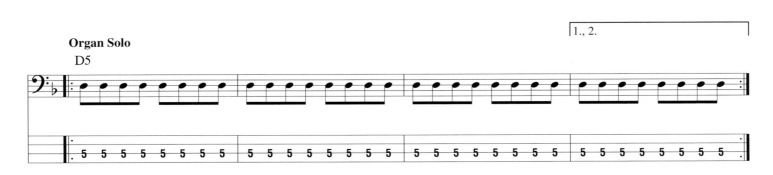

40

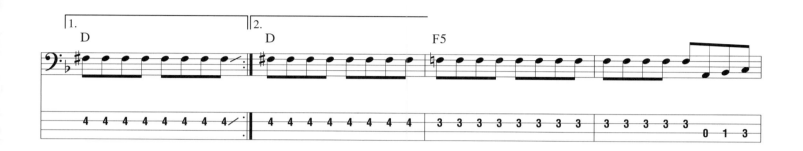

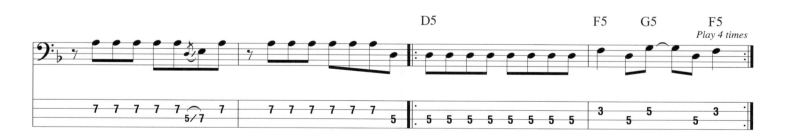

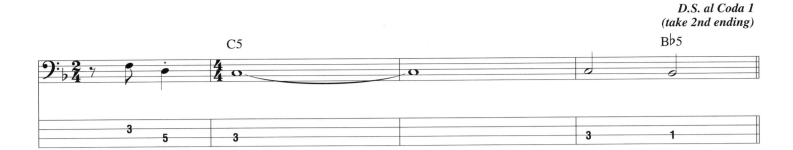

⊕ Coda 1

Guitar Solo

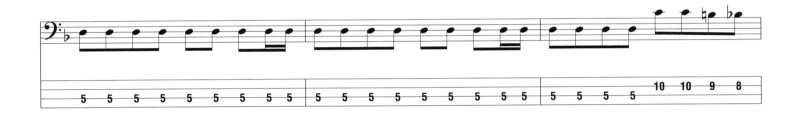

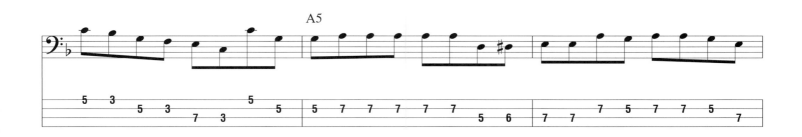
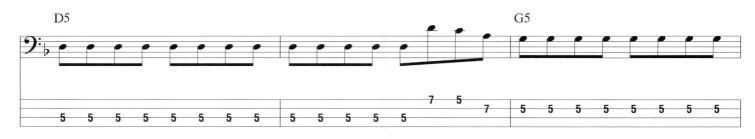

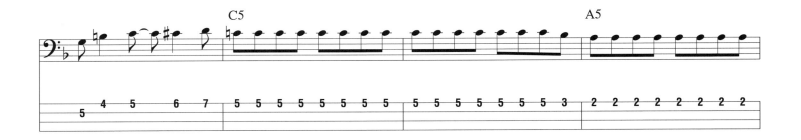

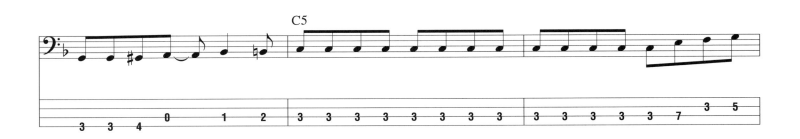

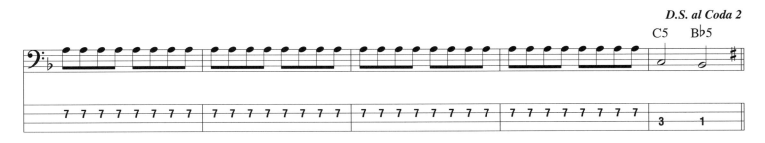

Additional Lyrics

2. A nobody gonna take my girl, I gonna keep her to the end.
   A nobody gonna have my girl, she stays close on ev'ry bend.
   Ooh, she's a killin' machine. She got a ev'rything.
   Like a movin' mouth, body control and ev'rything.
   I love her! I need her! I see her!
   Yeah, she turns me on!
   All right! Hold tight!
   I'm a highway star!

3. A nobody gonna take my head, I got speed inside my brain.
   A nobody gonna steal my head, now that I'm on the road again.
   Ooh, I'm in heaven again, I got a ev'rything.
   Like a movin' ground, an open road and ev'rything.
   I love her! I need her! I feel it!
   Eight cylinders, all mine!
   All right! Hold tight!
   I'm a highway star!

Mississippi Queen

Words and Music by Leslie West, Felix Pappalardi, Corky Laing and David Rea

she taught me   ev - 'ry - thing.

Verse

1. Way   down __

2. *See additional lyrics*

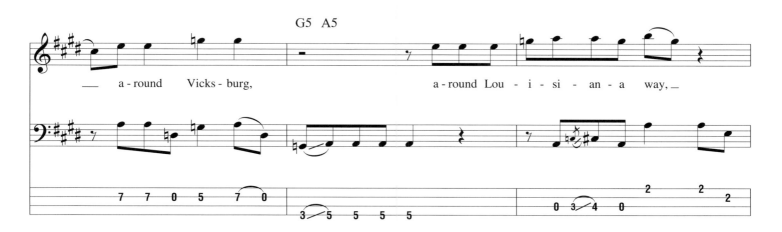

__ a - round   Vicks - burg,   a - round Lou - i - si - an - a   way, __

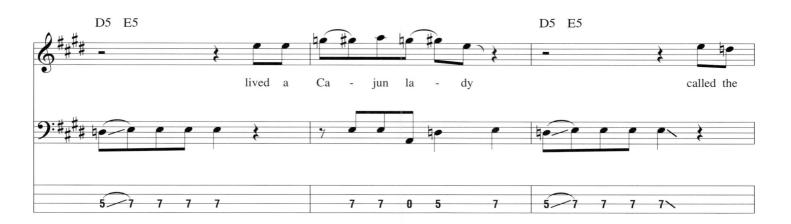

lived a   Ca - jun la - dy   called the

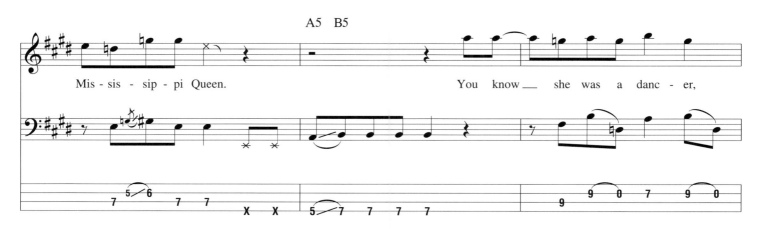

Mis - sis - sip - pi Queen.   You know __ she was a danc - er,

Additional Lyrics

2. This lady, she asked me if I would be her man.
   You know that I told her I'd do what I can
   To keep her lookin' pretty; buy her dresses that shine.
   While the rest of them dudes was a makin' their bread;
   Buddy, beg your pardon, I was losin' mine.

Suffragette City

Words and Music by David Bowie

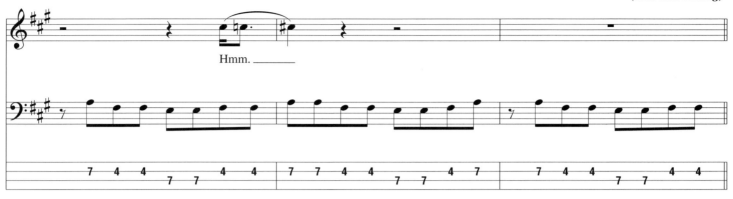

Hmm. _____

⊕ Coda

Guitar Solo

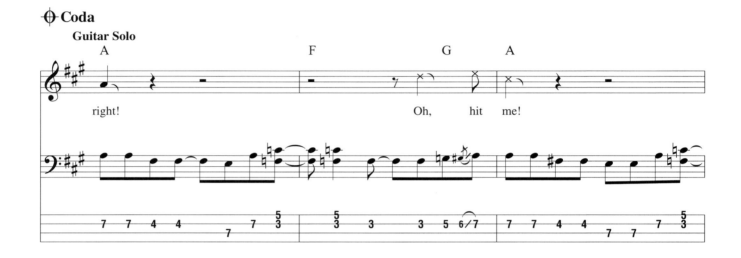

right!   Oh,   hit   me!

Chorus

Uh, don't ___ lean on me, man, 'cause you

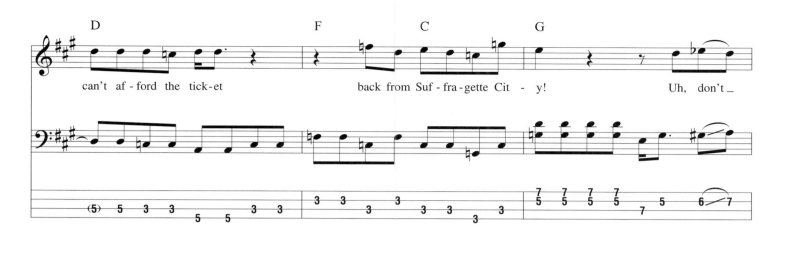

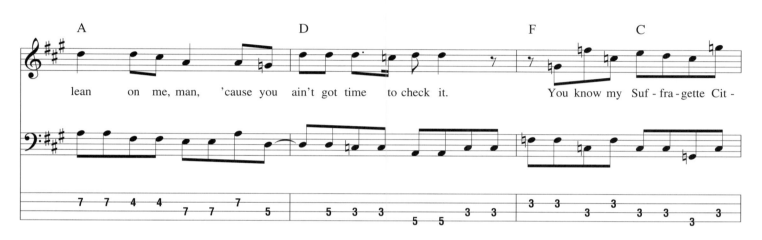

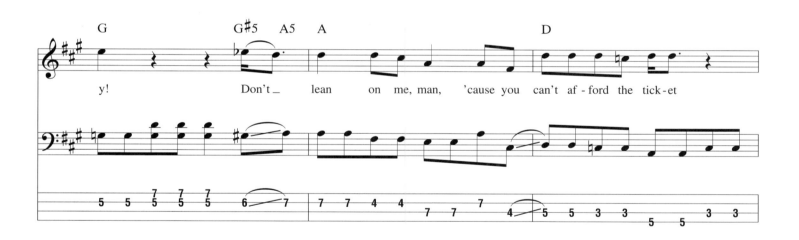

ain't got time to check it. You know my Suf-fra-gette Cit - y is out-ta

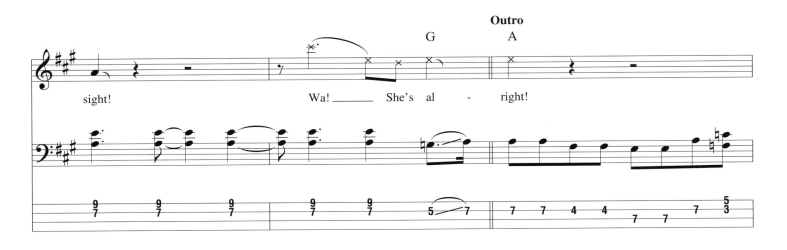

Outro

sight! Wa! _____ She's al - right!

My Suf-fra-gette Cit - y! My Suf-fra-gette Cit -

y! I'm back from Suf-fra-gette Cit - y!

Ah, _____ wham bam, thank you, ma'am!

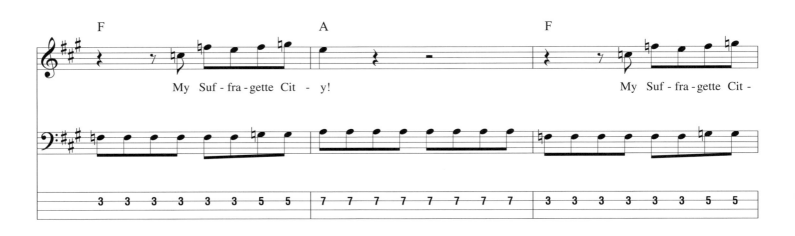

My Suf - fra - gette Cit - y!   My Suf - fra - gette Cit -

y!   Quite al - right! __ My Suf - fra - gette Cit - y!   Too _____ fine! __

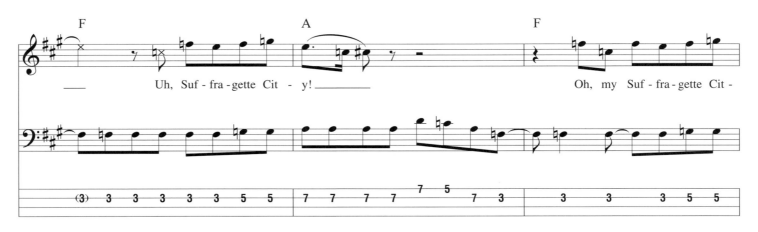

__ Uh, Suf - fra - gette Cit - y! _____   Oh, my Suf - fra - gette Cit -

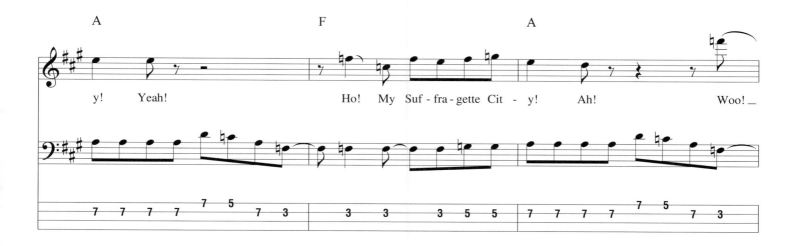

y! Yeah!   Ho! My Suf-fra-gette Cit - y!   Ah!   Woo!

My Suf-fra-gette Cit - y!   Ah, __ Suf-fra-gette...

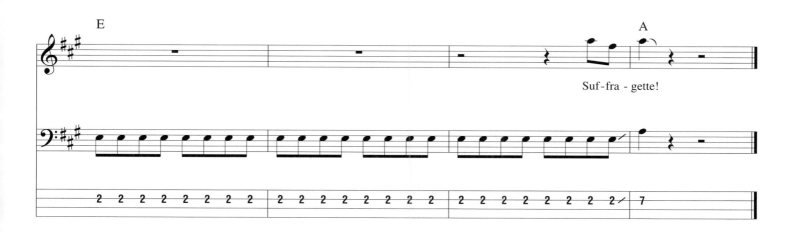

Suf-fra - gette!

Additional Lyrics

2. (Hey, man!) My school day's insane.
(Hey, man!) My work's down the drain.
(Hey, man!) Uh, she's a total blam blam,
She said she had to squeeze it but she... an' then she...

3. (Hey, man!) Ah, Henry, don't be unkind, go 'way!
(Hey, man!) I can't take you this time, no way.
(Hey, man!) Di-droogie, don't crash here.
There's only room for one an' here she comes, here she comes!

Train Kept A-Rollin'

Words and Music by Tiny Bradshaw, Lois Mann and Howie Kay

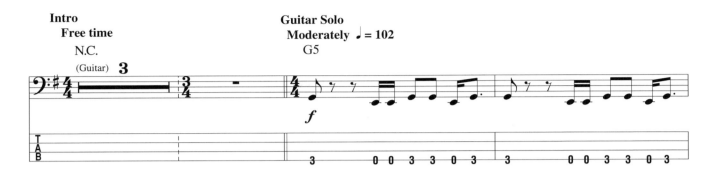

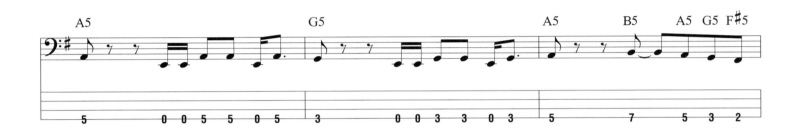

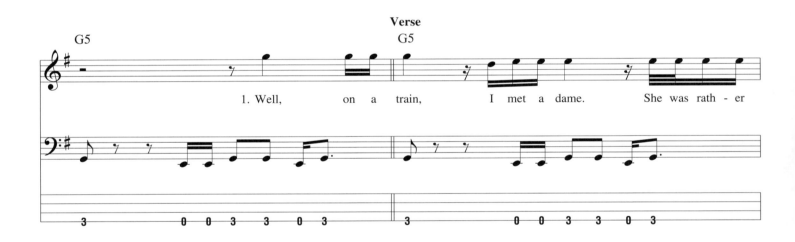

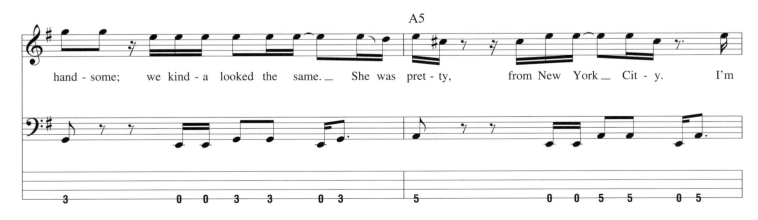

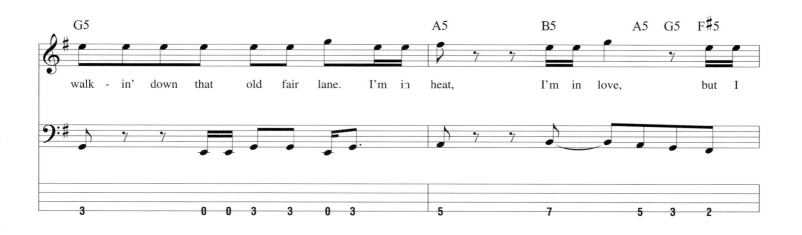

walk - in' down that old fair lane. I'm in heat, I'm in love, but I

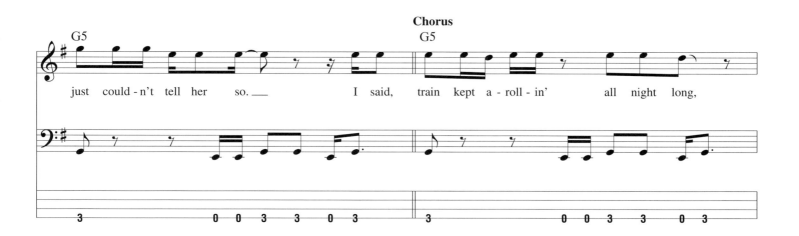

just could - n't tell her so. ___ I said, train kept a - roll - in' all night long,

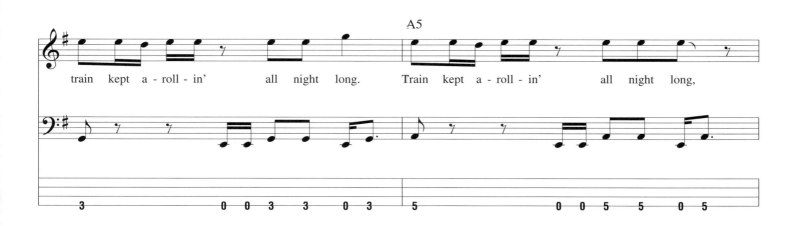

train kept a - roll - in' all night long. Train kept a - roll - in' all night long,

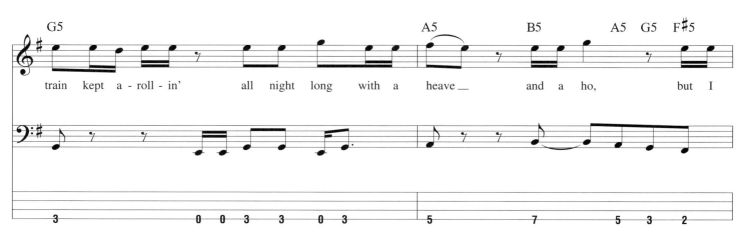

train kept a - roll - in' all night long with a heave ___ and a ho, but I

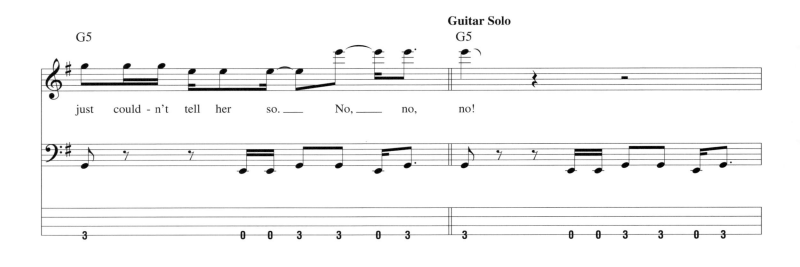

just could-n't tell her so.___ No,___ no,___ no!

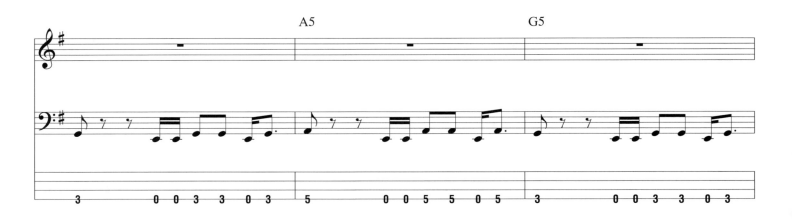

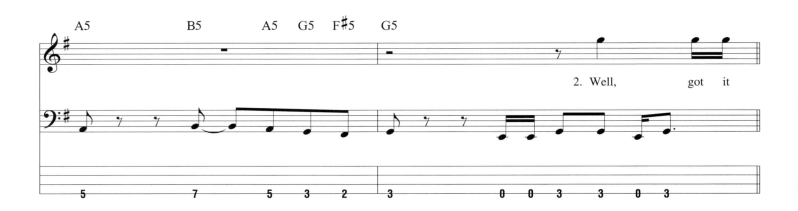

2. Well,___ got it

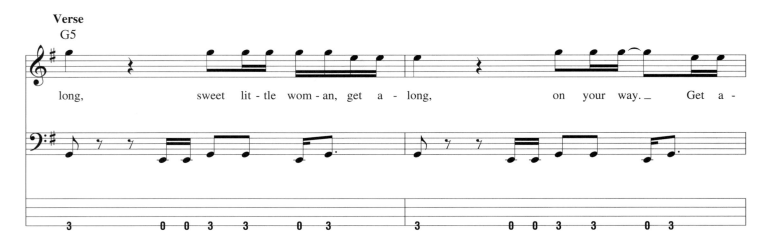

long,___ sweet lit-tle wom-an, get a- long,___ on your way.___ Get a-

long,   sweet lit - tle wom - an, get a - long, ___   on your way. __ I'm in

heat,   I'm in love,   but I just could - n't tell her so. ___   No, __ no,

Guitar Solo

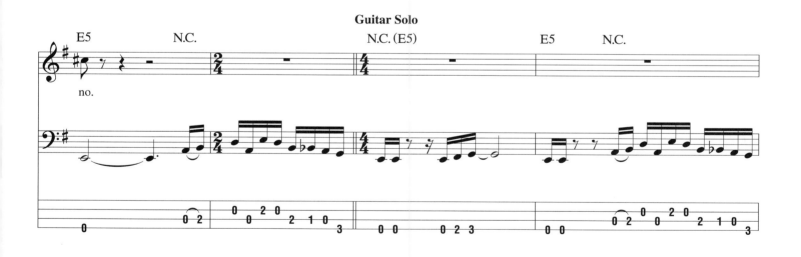

no.

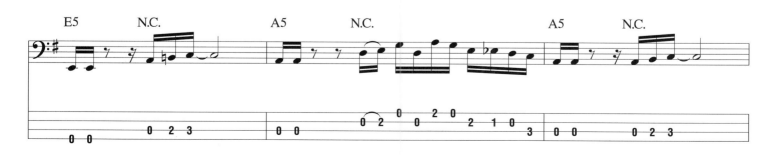

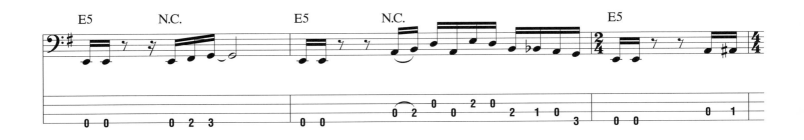

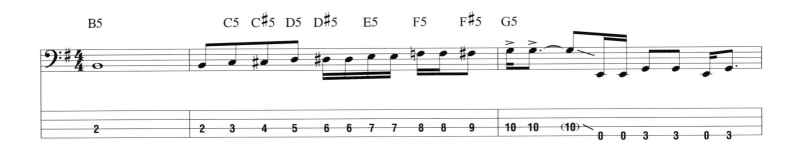

Interlude
Faster ♩ = 198
Bass tacet
(Snare drum & guitar)

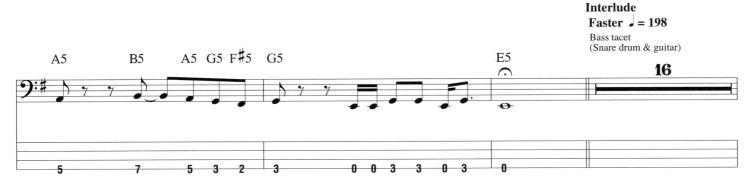

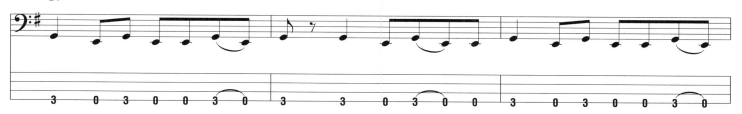

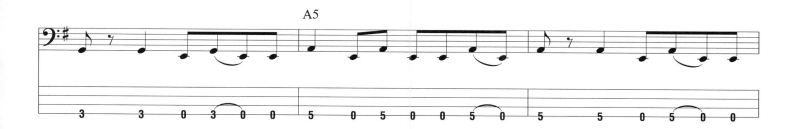

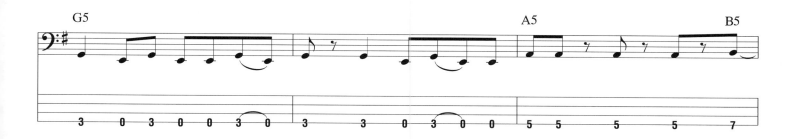

3. Yeah, on a

train, I met a dame. She was rath - er hand - some, we kind - a

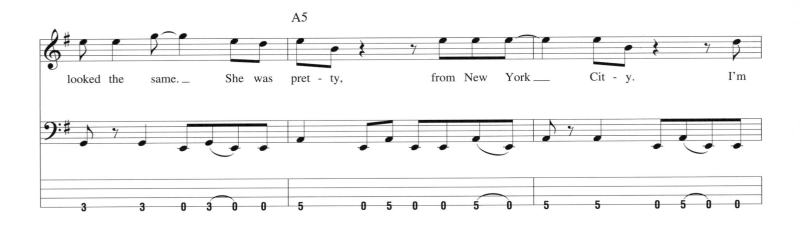

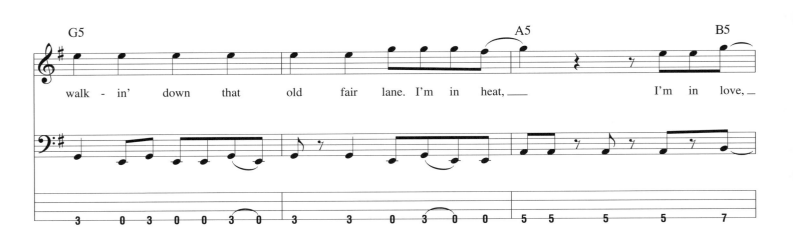

Chorus

A5

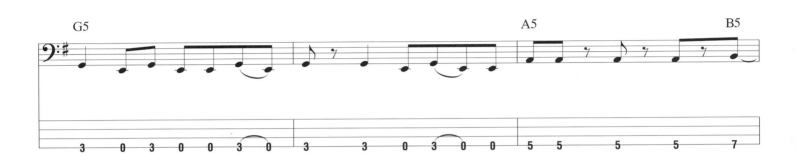

G5   A5   B5

A5   G5   F#5   G5

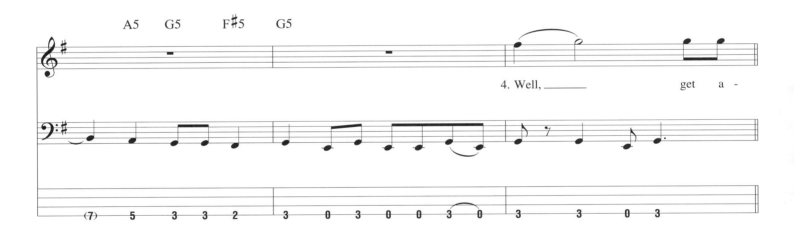

4. Well, _____ get a -

Verse
G5

long,   sweet   lit - tle wom - an, get a - long,

Guitar Solo

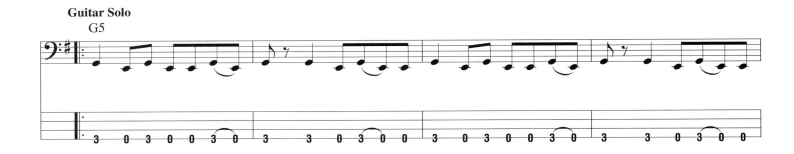

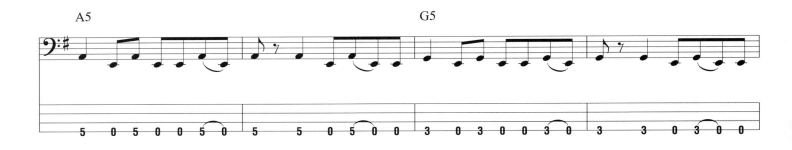

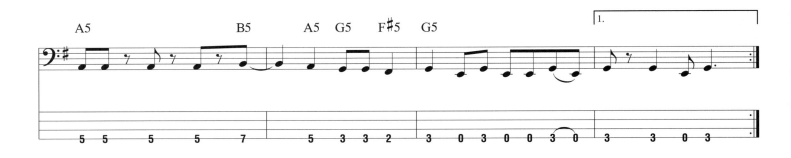

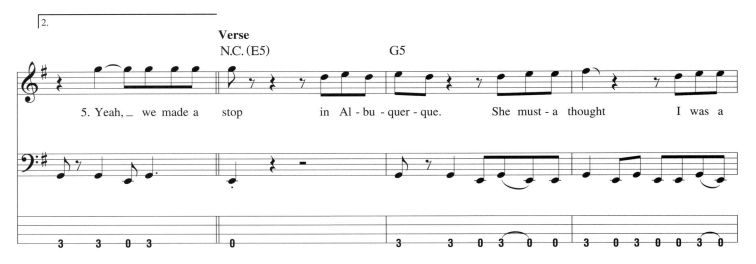

5. Yeah, __ we made a stop in Al - bu - quer - que. She must - a thought I was a

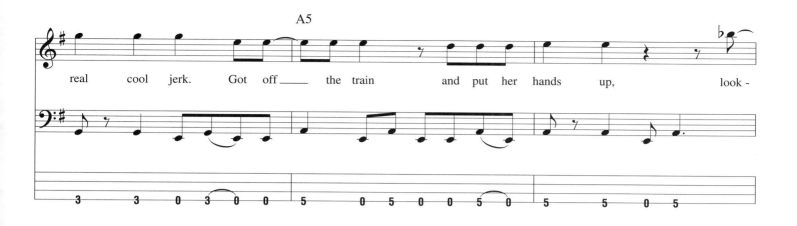

real cool jerk. Got off ____ the train and put her hands up, look-

-in' so good, I could-n't let her go. Oo, _____

____ but I just could-n't tell her so. ____ I said,

Chorus

train kept a-roll-in' all ____ night long, train kept a-roll-in'

70

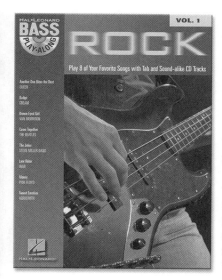

Hal•Leonard BASS PLAY•ALONG

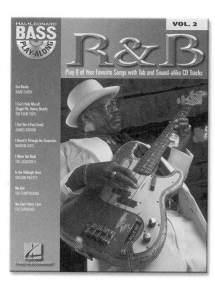

The Bass Play-Along Series will help you play your favorite songs quickly and easily! Just follow the tab, listen to the CD to hear how the bass should sound, and then play along using the separate backing tracks. The melody and lyrics are also included in the book in case you want to sing, or to simply help you follow along. The audio CD is playable on any CD player. For PC and Mac computer users, the CD is enhanced so you can adjust the recording to any tempo without changing pitch!

Rock VOLUME 1
Songs: Another One Bites the Dust • Badge • Brown Eyed Girl • Come Together • The Joker • Low Rider • Money • Sweet Emotion.
00699674 Book/CD Pack...$12.95

R&B VOLUME 2
Songs: Get Ready • I Can't Help Myself (Sugar Pie, Honey Bunch) • I Got You (I Feel Good) • I Heard It Through the Grapevine • I Want You Back • In the Midnight Hour • My Girl • You Can't Hurry Love.
00699675 Book/CD Pack...$12.95

Pop/Rock VOLUME 3
Songs: Crazy Little Thing Called Love • Crocodile Rock • Maneater • My Life • No Reply at All • Peg • Message in a Bottle • Suffragette City.
00699677 Book/CD Pack...$12.95

'90s Rock VOLUME 4
Songs: All I Wanna Do • Fly Away • Give It Away • Hard to Handle • Jeremy • Know Your Enemy • Spiderwebs • You Oughta Know.
00699679 Book/CD Pack...$12.95

Funk VOLUME 5
Songs: Brick House • Cissy Strut • Get Off • Get Up (I Feel Like Being) a Sex Machine • Higher Ground • Le Freak • Pick up the Pieces • Super Freak.
00699680 Book/CD Pack...$12.95

Classic Rock VOLUME 6
Songs: Free Ride • Funk #49 • Gimme Three Steps • Green-Eyed Lady • Radar Love • Werewolves of London • White Room • Won't Get Fooled Again.
00699678 Book/CD Pack...$12.95

Hard Rock VOLUME 7
Songs: Crazy Train • Detroit Rock City • Iron Man • Livin' on a Prayer • Living After Midnight • Peace Sells • Smoke on the Water • The Trooper.
00699676 Book/CD Pack...$12.95

Prices, contents and availability subject to change without notice.

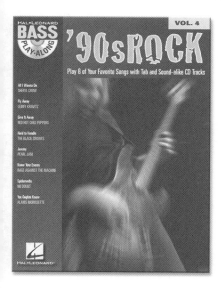

FOR MORE INFORMATION,
SEE YOUR LOCAL MUSIC DEALER,
OR WRITE TO:

HAL•LEONARD®
CORPORATION
7777 W. BLUEMOUND RD. P.O. BOX 13819
MILWAUKEE, WISCONSIN 53213
Visit Hal Leonard Online at **www.halleonard.com**

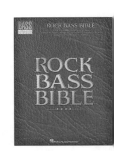
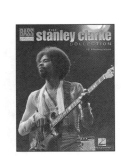